The six 'pillars' for developing thinking

According to the King's College cognitive model, there are : crucial to effective learning. These will be considered in tur associated *assessment for learning* strategies where appro to think of these as sequential, although there is an implied sequence. but metacognition and bridging in particular need to be encouraged whenever the opportunity arises.)

1. Tuning in *(Concrete Preparation)*

Debra Myhill (Myhill, D. et al 2006: 97) has demonstrated that learners sometimes leave lessons more confused about the concepts being taught than when they arrived. Low achievement by some boys in particular can be attributed to the fact that they do not link the new knowledge to their existing understanding. All too often the only links made are to school knowledge rather than the learners' own wider understanding. Making explicit links to existing concepts and patterns of thinking in the brain is essential – otherwise the new learning is built on sand. Some new learning simply sits alongside the old ideas, with no real engagement with any existing preconceptions. This may result in learners simultaneously believing completely contradictory ideas.

For example, a teacher may use the term 'scale'. This term has completely different meanings in different subject areas:
Art/ CDT – scale up, scale down, scale drawing, scale model
Biology – scales on a fish, snake etc.
Business Studies – salary scale, sliding scale, economy of scale
Food Technology – scale in a kettle etc.
Geography – scale of a map, Beaufort scale, Richter scale
Geology – time scale
Maths – measuring scale, vertical scale on a graph, decimal scale
Media/ English – scale a fence, mountain etc.
Music – musical scale, chromatic scale
Physics – weighing scales, temperature scales

Of course the meanings of some of these terms overlap. But it is easy to imagine many cases where the learner misinterprets what the teacher is saying in the case of *scale*, to take just this one example. In some cases words used will have additional meanings outside the school context.

The misinterpretation is almost certainly invisible to the teacher. Unless the learner is asked to explain particular terms in their own way, the teacher may not know until a 'howler' appears in some written work. It would be far better if we could find ways to ensure that the misconceptions are explored and confronted as soon as possible.

It is helpful to remember Bakhtin's argument (1981) that we do not learn new words out of dictionaries but out of other people's mouths. It takes time to assimilate a new word as we gradually refine our understanding until we can use that new word confidently and appropriately ourselves. If learner and teacher mean the same thing when using a particular word, the lesson will clearly have greater impact.

Tuning in is vital, both at the level of understanding terminology and at the level of understanding concepts etc. In the King's College model of thinking this is referred to as **concrete preparation**. *"The first part of the intervention involves 'concrete preparation'. This is the stage in which the scene is set and the situation is explained to the children. ... unfamiliar words and phrases are introduced to them."*
[The Standards Site – what is Cognitive Intervention all about?]

Knowing what a good result looks like

A closely related concept to concrete preparation in **assessment for learning** (**AfL**) is that learners need to understand what constitutes success in this particular topic area. The two main ways for teachers to achieve this are:

❖ generating success criteria through whole class teacher-led discussion
❖ looking at an example of quality in groups/ as a whole class and extracting/ teasing out exactly what the qualities are.

The two strategies can of course be combined.

A striking feature of assessment for learning research is that learners with low basic skills scores seem to make significantly greater strides than those with high basic skills scores. [The chart opposite shows before and after averages after an AfL intervention for pupils with low (left hand column), medium (middle column) and high (right hand column) basic skills scores.] This can be partly caused by the problem of diminishing returns in raising the achievement of already high scoring learners. But another very significant factor is that one of the reasons low achievers are not achieving is that they are not at all clear exactly what constitutes success, and are therefore to an extent working in the dark.

Knowing what constitutes success in a particular area can be considered just as crucial in terms of **tuning in** or **concrete preparation** as words and phrases etc.

2. Challenge *(Cognitive Conflict)*

"The teacher presents the pupils with a situation which they cannot tackle with their existing cognitive structure. This is the first stage of the intervention activities. It is described as cognitive conflict, which is usually taken to mean cognitive challenge." [The Standards Site – what is Cognitive Intervention all about?]

Differentiation *can* be interpreted as providing work at the level the learner is working at. The danger if this happens is that it will confirm the learner at the level of the status quo and not help them to move forward. The results in the charts opposite suggest that some learners could be challenged far more than they are. Indeed, since these are average scores, some of the learners may well cope with challenges above the highest scores indicated. The multiplier effect is clearly working here.

A useful term here is the *zone of potential development* (**ZPD**). When a learner is given a test such as the Binet test, it establishes a measure of that learner's unaided 'ability'. However, the psychologist can then go on to discuss with the child why certain answers have been given, and discuss various wrong answers – trying to establish the thinking patterns, and helping the child move forward. Retesting the learner after this discussion provides a second score. The difference between the two scores can be considered as the zone of potential development – the area in which a teacher should ideally work. (Shayer and Adey 2002: 183)
The second chart opposite suggests the zone of potential development for the learners in the AfL intervention.

Of course all children will have different ZPDs, which may at first seem an insuperable problem in a mixed ability classroom – or even in a class that is set. This is where the next 'pillar' comes in (see **Talk** below).

Wrong answers valued

One of the most significant factors in learning is how far learners feel secure in the classroom – the classroom ethos. If learners feel they may be ridiculed by other learners, they are far less likely to offer answers, speculate or engage in any task. If,

The Multiplier Effect in Teaching © **Michael Ross 2008**

Basic Skills and potential 1

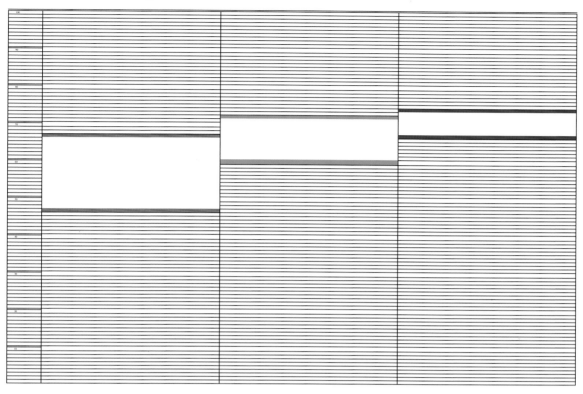

Average percentage scores before and after AfL intervention grouped by basic skills scores.
Based on data from Frederiksen, J., and White, B. (1997) quoted in James, M. (2007)

Basic Skills and potential 2

Inferred *zones of potential development* for learners involved in AfL intervention.
Based on data from Frederiksen, J., and White, B. (1997) quoted in James, M. (2007)

however, an atmosphere has been created in which wrong answers are genuinely valued and explored, learners will steadily feel more confident in allowing their real thought processes out into the open. This strategy from assessment for learning links closely with *challenge,* as learners are having their existing thought patterns deliberately questioned. (One way of interpreting some of Socrates' dialogues is that he was constantly exploring wrong answers rather than giving 'right' answers.)

In some schools posters around the classroom suggest, for example, that if you always get the answer right you are not being challenged enough/ you are not challenging yourself enough - and you are not actually learning anything. If all the questions teachers ask elicit the right answer, this is presumably a clear indication that the questions are not challenging enough. The interesting issue arises – what is the optimal number of right answers? "We can learn from each other's wrong answers" as a poster in the classroom is a good starting point.

King's College research has shown that right answers can be right for the wrong reason. Wrong answers give an insight into what needs to be explained and taught. A learner who gets the answer wrong and doesn't know why suffers a 'double whammy'. They thought their answer was right – and now may well not know why it was wrong or how they can make a successful attempt next time.

Some teachers have found that a very successful strategy is to keep asking 'why?' Mike Hughes has suggested that the difference between a good teacher and a very good teacher is that the very good teacher keeps asking the pupils why. This will clearly generate cognitive conflict as the learners are forced to think more and more deeply about a particular idea.

Ladders not Labels
One of the most dramatic findings from assessment for learning is that formative feedback produces far greater gains than summative 'feedback'. Even if formative feedback is given, any simultaneous summative feedback will drown out the benefits of the formative comments. Once a learner has a 'label' as Level 3 or Grade E, whether imposed by the teacher or by themselves, that label will to some extent be self-confirming.

In terms of challenge, the teacher has the very tricky task of finding just the right feedback to move the learner on to the next step on the ladder of progress. (Even more demanding is to support learners in giving each other clear and helpful advice for moving on, leading to effective self-assessment and independent learning.)

For assessment to be formative it is necessary that the learner actually makes an improvement. A specific time-slot in the lesson needs to be set aside for the learner to make a specific change and improvement. One reason low achievers benefit so much from this process may well be motivational. Every time they make an incremental improvement, they can see that their performance has improved AND that they themselves have been responsible for that improvement. Changing to an internal 'locus of control' provides the learner with an inbuilt multiplier effect.

The often quoted 'three stars and a wish' is misleading. One definition of 'star' is 'reward for good work'. The aim of the 'star' here is not to *reward* but to give precise feedback about the strategies they are using that they should continue to use. Dweck (2007) suggests some praise can lead to 'a short burst of pride followed by a long string of negative consequences'. In contrast, praise for *strategies* fosters motivation. One definition of 'wish' is 'to desire, especially vainly or helplessly that something were the case'. (Chambers) The word clearly has associations which are not at all helpful! What is actually needed is a specific *action* or *change* which improves the quality of the performance/ writing/ speaking/ thought process etc.

3. Talk *(Social Construction)*

"This is a social activity in which the children are encouraged to discuss the problem with one another, to try to solve it together. The teacher's role is to mediate while the pupils construct the knowledge and understanding."
[The Standards Site – what is Cognitive Intervention all about?]

In the Binet test experiment referred to above, it was the adult who engaged in discussion. However, it can be equally or more productive for the learner to engage in discussion with a peer. Many insights are made when a learner is working with someone who has an understanding just ahead of their own, and can express it in terms their peer can easily follow. It has been calculated by Michael Shayer of King's College, London, that 80% of what learners learn they learn from each other rather than the teacher. (Of course the 20% high quality teacher input is the essential ingredient if the 80% learner to learner interaction is to be productive and successful.)

Within the six pillars, this element is referred to as **social construction**. It is a *social* activity and it involves the *construction* of new patterns of thinking. It has been suggested that explaining to others is some 100 times as powerful as having something explained to you. Intuitively this sounds quite conceivable because we have all experienced being half way through an explanation and realizing we have not thoroughly understood the issue, or being asked a question and realizing we can't answer it clearly or fully. Explaining to others reveals the gaps in our own understanding and what we need to explore further, *particularly* when we are questioned about a topic. This is another promising area for a multiplier effect.

Often in pairings the 'middle ability' learners lose out as they are neither explaining nor being explained to. Research by King's College suggests that pairing half the 'middle' with the 'top' and half the 'middle' with the 'bottom' may be the most productive strategy.

In terms of assessment for learning, some questioning techniques can help learners explore ideas more fully. For example, if the teacher has a strategy of 'basketball not ping-pong' in which learners may be asked to comment on a peer's answer, each learner can build on the ideas of the previous speakers, perhaps exploring which of two previous answers they consider more accurate or helpful. If the teacher adopts a ping-pong approach of *teacher question – single pupil answer* the rest of the class is less likely to be fully engaged, and genuine social construction will almost certainly not take place. However, there is also a place for an extended series of questions to a single learner, challenging them to develop their ideas more and more deeply.

Random pairs
A related strategy from **assessment for learning** is random pairs. Neil Mercer and Karen Littleton suggest that learners can all too easily become lazy in their friendship groups and consciously or unconsciously make a pact not to challenge each other too much. "Particularly when groups of friends worked together, the discussions were uncritical, involving only superficial consideration and acceptance of each other's ideas." (Mercer and Littleton, 2007, p.58) ['Lollipop' sticks with learner names on them can be used, with learners choosing a random partner. When learners *know* that the teacher does not manipulate the groupings, they cease trying to work out why they have been allocated to a particular partner etc., with clear benefits in application and motivation.]

On the other hand, if learners have to engage with the brain power and thinking patterns of some 29 other learners, it is inevitable that they will have to engage with a

7

wider repertoire of language and thinking. This in itself is beneficial, and introduces a multiplier effect. But another crucial benefit is in terms of the ability of different learners to engage with each other socially, often finding that those they had spoken to little or not at all in fact were more interesting human beings than they had realized. In some cases, very isolated and quiet learners have become far more sociable and more able to interact with a range of others as a result of this strategy.

Ground rules for talk

As teachers know all too well, successful talk without teacher intervention does not come easily. However, if learners establish rules for talk on the lines suggested by Neil Mercer before a particular activity, they tend to be far more focused – and willing to obey their own rules! (Mercer, 2000, p.28)

Speaking frames

In 2007 the Basic Skills Agency in Wales arranged for SMT observations of learners with low basic skills in primary and secondary classes. A striking finding was that problems were most likely to arise in subjects other than Welsh (second language) or MFL. The reason seems to be that in the language lessons the teachers assumed the learners would not have the necessary language patterns and therefore provided models. In the other subjects, no such support was given.

Yet how do we expect learners to internalize the many different language patterns required in the range of subjects taught if the patterns are not explicitly established? Many teachers now use speaking frames along the lines suggested by Sue Palmer and Pie Corbett (2003: 66). If all learners speak one relevant complete sentence based on the given patterns out loud, each learner will begin to internalize the necessary technical vocabulary, appropriate connectives and language patterns for that particular topic, and be far more ready to speak or write fluently on the topic. This is a powerful way to embed valuable language patterns in a very clear and focused way – another clear example of a potential multiplier factor.

Examples of speaking frame sentence openers

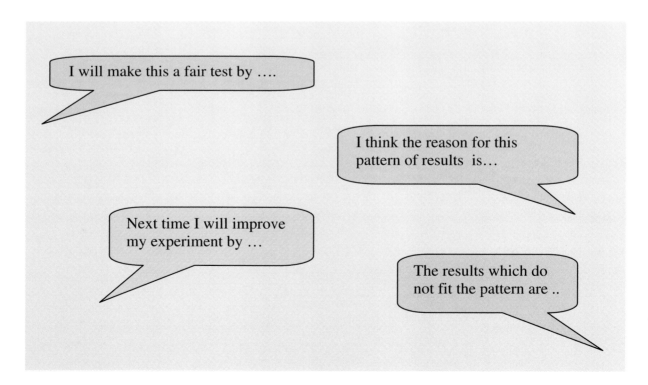

The Multiplier Effect in Teaching © **Michael Ross 2008**

4. Thinking about thinking, learning about learning *(Metacognition)*

"Metacognition is the conscious reflection by a child on his or her own thinking processes, often (but not always) after he or she has worked through a given problem. In this way the pupils become aware of their own reasoning, and the thinking process becomes explicit."
[The Standards Site – what is Cognitive Intervention all about?]

If a learner considers implicitly or explicitly that each element in their school life needs to be learnt as a separate piece of information, the prospect is so daunting that it would not be surprising if the individual gave up the attempt. However, if learners appreciate that they are learning *strategies* that can be used in a range of situations, they come to appreciate that each strategy has a multiplier effect of its own.   (For example by understanding text purposes – see page 11.) Equally, if they can track back to how they solved a particular problem, they are in a much stronger position to follow a successful route on a future occasion.

In terms of **assessment for learning,** metacognition may well occur when learners assess their own or their peer's work against the success criteria. (See page 18.) They will need to establish how far they have achieved a successful outcome. But it is vital that the success criteria should not be seen as fixed in stone. Learners can also explore how far the success criteria generated at the outset in fact match the successful outcomes they can now study. It may well be that some learners have taken unconventional, but successful, routes. In this sense the often used phrase 'closing the gap' is not helpful, as it implies a fixed end point rather than an open ended exploration of possible alternative routes to success.

Strategies not Solutions
If a learner is given an answer to something they are struggling over, this may well provide a short-term solution, but will almost certainly not help their deeper or longer-term learning. As a simple example, if a learner asks how to spell *practice/ practise* in a given context and is simply told by the teacher or LSA which to use in this instance without explanation, their learning is no further forward.

However, if they are encouraged to compare it with *advice/ advise*, where you can **hear** the difference in spelling between the noun and the verb, they have a strategy they can use in every subject, and in fact throughout their lives, for *advice/ advise, practice/ practise, licence/ license* etc. Another example of the multiplier factor.

If learners are regularly helped to establish *strategies* rather than being given *solutions*, they will become more independent learners and more successful learners. However, they need to know which strategy to use in a given context, so it is *'metacognition about strategies, rather than the strategies themselves, that appears to be essential'.* (Sternberg, 1998, p.128) Again to take the simple example of *practice/ practise*, the strategy mentioned above is no use for spelling *Wednesday*!

Questionnaires
Over the past few years the Vale of Glamorgan School Improvement Service has been filming examples of assessment for learning and developing thinking in action in the classroom. This has included interviews with learners. A striking finding has been that learners who have been given questionnaires about the approaches being used have been the most articulate about the approaches and how far they have found them useful; and the impact of the learning experiences has been multiplied.

9

The questionnaires were designed as part of the evaluation of the action research. It became evident that they were not a neutral part of the process! The very act of filling in the questionnaire made it more likely that the learners thought about the different learning and teaching approaches, why they were being used, and how far each approach suited their own learning needs. The questionnaires can be considered part of the process of metacognition – learners thinking about their learning and what processes in the classroom worked for them. Indeed since metacognition is one of the six pillars, it might seem strange if learners did *not* benefit from a questionnaire about the learning strategies they are using.

Sample questionnaire for learners					
* = I am not at all confident about this/ this is not true					
**** = I am very confident about this / this is almost always true					
	Statement	*	**	***	****
1	I am given time to think before answering some questions.				
2	I listen to the answers from other pupils.				
3	I sometimes comment on what another pupil has said.				
4	I try to guess what answer the teacher wants.				
5	I work out what I think is the best answer.				
6	I think up an answer of my own every time a question is asked.				
7	Other pupils find the comments I make to them helpful.				
8	I find the comments other pupils make to me helpful.				
9	I learn from the wrong answers of other pupils.				
10	I learn from my own wrong answers.				
What helped me most was… because…					
What helped me least was… because…					

5. Linking the learning *(Bridging)*

Concrete preparation (the first pillar discussed) can be considered bridging *from* learners' existing knowledge and experience. Within the six pillars **bridging** refers to times in the lesson when links are explicitly made to other subjects in the school/ other areas of life where the same principles or strategies might apply. This can occur at any point in the lesson. As mentioned in the section on Concrete Preparation, if these links are not made the learning may be shallow or even retrogressive. (Any use of similes or metaphors almost inevitably involves some sort of bridging from the new to the familiar.)

The Multiplier Effect in Teaching © **Michael Ross 2008**

To take one example, *evaluation* is often found to be a difficult area for learners in CDT, English, History and ICT. If learners see how evaluation in one subject can inform evaluation in another, their learning is far more powerful and efficient. Using the Sue Palmer *discussion* skeleton for evaluation in all subjects, with appropriate variations, can make the point very strongly that similar structures and connectives are useful in all these cases. This links strongly to the sixth pillar.

	The six non-fiction text purposes with Sue Palmer skeletons		
	Text purpose		**Useful connectives etc. for this text purpose – add your own useful words for each**
1	Recount *this is what happened*	what happened, in time sequence	*Seriation, chronology, sequencing of past events, time sequence* Then... After that... Meanwhile... Simultaneously, Before... The next/following day... By the time...
2	Instruction *this is what you need to do*	what to do, in time sequence	*Chronology, ordering, but for future event* First... Second... etc., Next... After that... Meanwhile, While... in... on... by... next to... from... to...
3	Information *these are the important facts*	by categories/ subheadings	*Classification, sorting (+ comparison/ evaluation)* in... at... on... for... also... except... for example, only... (who, when, where, why, what, how?)
4	Explanation *this is why it happens/ happened*	causes and effects	*Reasoning, justifying, asking why, causality* because... so that... by... in order to... As a result, Consequently, This causes... Therefore... If... then...
5	Persuasion *this is what you should think/ believe*	for and why not against *or* against and why not for	*Evaluation, reasoning based on 'subjective' opinion* because... Consequently, Nevertheless, As a result, First, Also, In conclusion,
6	Discussion *this is what people think/ say about ...*	for and against + conclusion	*Evaluation, reasoning based on 'objective' opinion; conservation (of volume etc. in science), points of view* Some people say... On the other hand, However, because... Therefore, whereas... Alternatively, From this point of view... From that point of view... the same, different, more, less, opposite

11

The Multiplier Effect in Teaching © **Michael Ross 2008**

6. Making explicit the type of thinking being used (*Schemata*)

The sixth pillar relates to the type of thinking which is central in any particular teaching activity. For example an activity might involve sequencing or classification or causality or evaluation. The Sue Palmer text purpose symbols can be used here as well, since these also relate to the types of thinking involved. *Recount* involves sequencing events and includes seriation, *information* requires classification, *explanation* involves causality, *discussion* involves evaluation and perspective taking and so on. As has been suggested, if all subject areas employ these text purpose diagrams, whenever possible, it helps learners to see links between different subject areas (contributing to *concrete preparation* and *bridging*). The connectives regularly used in each text purpose (see page 11) also provide the key to the types of language and thinking required. A learner can use the connective *whereas,* for example, in a spoken or written sentence, to evaluate the difference between two texts/ performances/ objects etc.

Knowing the text purpose helps learners to know what type of thinking they are expected to employ; it helps learners to know what connectives to use; and it helps learners to link their learning in one subject area with their learning in another subject area.

It could be argued that this is too elaborate. But at its heart is the simple idea that learners should know the kind of thought processes they need to engage in to be successful in a particular activity. It would seem strange and illogical not to give them support and clarity in this absolutely fundamental area – the *way* they are expected to use their brains in this particular context. It could well help to define a 'big question' for the current focus of work for a class.

30 strategies which include a multiplier effect

The following chart provides 30 different strategies for improving learning and teaching. In each case the reason for using the strategy is provided in brief, but in many cases this booklet provides a fuller rationale. As suggested earlier, it is vital that the teacher understands as fully as possible why the strategy may work.

Assessment for Learning/ developing thinking strategies

	Strategy	Why it may be effective
	Quality of talk	
1	Learners help generate success criteria.	If learners are actively involved in generating success criteria, e.g. looking at work by a pupil from a previous year, they will understand more clearly and actively what makes for success – and are more likely to achieve success.
2	No hands up. Mini-whiteboards.	To increase thinking time. Most learners, including adults, can give a longer and more thoughtful response if given time to think. Time should also be allowed at end of a learner's answer, encouraging a fuller/ deeper response.
3	Think, pair, share. Mini-whiteboards.	Expressing our ideas to others helps us to formulate these ideas. It is less intimidating to present ideas on behalf of a pair than being totally responsible yourself. Answers on mini-whiteboards can be easily removed – reducing anxiety.
4	Poker face.	Learners genuinely say what they think/ believe rather than working out from body language what the teacher *wants* to hear. The learner grapples with the *task* rather than trying to guess what the teacher expects.

5	Basketball not ping-pong.	Learners have to listen to fellow learners' answers if they may have to respond to them! An immediate teacher response (yes/no) will usually shut thought down/ close an enquiring mind.
6	Random partners.	Friendship groups tend to develop a cosy familiarity that is unchallenging. Engaging with a full range of brains is powerful. Learners will not be distracted by trying to work out why the teacher has chosen a particular grouping.
7	Learners generate own questions on topic.	Learners will be highly motivated to find answers to their own questions, and these are *genuine* questions. The questions asked also reveal what learners already know/ need to know.
8	Wrong answers valued.	Mistakes and misunderstandings are a powerful route to real understanding: locating and eliminating misconceptions means new understanding is built on solid foundations. If fear of failure is reduced, learning opportunities increase.
9	Learners explain to each other.	Explaining to others can be 100 times more powerful than having it explained to you. Some 80% of what learners learn comes from their peers.
10	Keep asking *why?*	Learners need to be challenged to take their understanding one step further. Learners should develop the habit of asking each other *why?* Explaining to others is powerful!
Use of feedback/ quality of feedback		
11	Early/ ongoing/ regular feedback.	Valuable learning time is lost if learners go down a wrong track before any intervention. 5 minutes in (or even less) may be a good first time.
12	Feedback based on success criteria.	The feedback should be explicitly linked to the agreed success criteria, otherwise the focus is lost.
13	Peer and self evaluation.	Peer feedback against the success criteria at various points in the process sharpens the focus and judgement of both learners. Whenever a peer becomes a 'teacher', the impact of the learning is increased. Ongoing self-assessment keeps the learning on track.
14	Three achievements + one action point.	Learners need to know what they are doing that they need to carry on doing and consolidate. But they also need to know precisely how they can take a step forward. This next step needs to be clearly expressed, based on the success criteria, and something they can definitely act on.
15	Action taken then and there.	Assessment only becomes formative when the learner actually makes a significant improvement. Learners benefit from the realization that they have improved their own performance. Shifting to an internal locus of control (believing they are responsible for their own learning) is one of the most powerful changes that can occur.
16	No marks or grades on work, but in mark book.	Marks and grades are a complete distraction from learning. Learners need to focus on the quality of their performance, not comparing their mark/ grade with others. *Teachers* need to track how learners are progressing, for example highlighting the *criteria* achieved at a particular time.

The Multiplier Effect in Teaching © **Michael Ross 2008**

	Sharing criteria with learners	
17	Separating skill from context.	Learners need to focus on the skills that can be used elsewhere, **not** on the particular context. e.g. information writing not recipe writing; how they solved a problem, not the specific answer. This increases the impact of the learning.
18	Ladders not labels.	The criteria by which their performance is judged must not be a secret. Learners need to know where they are (in terms of criteria for success) and what their next step(s) should be.
19	Using exemplars.	If learners analyse the performance of others, they will begin the necessary process of internalizing the success criteria. They can then build on this knowledge in their own performance.
20	Evaluating success criteria.	Success criteria need to be seen as provisional – having completed the task, do we need to adjust our criteria?
	Peer and self assessment	
21	Traffic lights.	Learners evaluate how confident they feel at any point in the lesson/ about a topic/ about an answer they are giving. Invaluable feedback to the teacher; learners can give tentative answers with more confidence.
22	Peer assessment first?	Peer assessment is often a necessary stage before learners can be confident in self-assessment. It is easier to be objective about others.
23	Self assessment as aim.	Self-assessment is essential if learners are to be independent and autonomous – the ultimate goal.
24	Exploring how answers were reached.	If learners regularly think about the way they have tackled a problem, they will become far more aware of their own thinking strategies and how to be more effective learners.
25	Learning about learning.	Learners need to explore the strategies they have used that have been most powerful: *metacognition*. Also, they need to explore where they can use these elsewhere: *bridging* – not seeing each subject as isolated.
26	Questionnaires.	If learners are asked about particular strategies, they will be more self-aware about the strategies and more reflective about the ways they learn most effectively.
	Developing thinking	
27	Text purposes used + Sue Palmer skeletons.	Learners gain confidence by knowing that there are just 6 basic non-fiction text purposes rather than a bewildering range across many subject areas.
28	Connectives identified and used.	The connectives provide the key to the kinds of thinking required in this area. The combination of text purpose and suitable connectives is fundamental to understanding reading, and to the process of writing.
29	Exploring strategies not giving solutions.	*Solutions* tend to be one-off and limited. *Strategies* can be used in a range of contexts and are far more powerful for learning.
30	Exploring the strategies learners use.	There may be valid alternatives to a teacher's preferred strategy which some learners grasp more easily. Different learners learn in different ways.

The Multiplier Effect in Teaching   © **Michael Ross 2008**

The chart on this page is an attempt to bring all six 'pillars' into an overview, suggesting some powerful strategies linked to each pillar. It should be emphasized that these pillars are not (necessarily) sequential (it is not a five part lesson) but that any 'pillar' can be paramount at any stage in the development of a lesson.
Note: cognitive conflict is often (but not always) tackled by using social construction.

Not the five part lesson + strategies
(*Speaking frames* can be useful in social construction, metacognition and bridging.)

Developing Thinking	Strategies	Other sources of strategies
Schemata *What kinds of thinking?*	Make explicit the kind of thinking required – sort, classify, evaluate etc. 6 text purposes + connectives.	 *Literacy*
Concrete Preparation *Tuning in.*	Prepare the ground in advance. Traffic lighting to find what they already know. Recall + reframe. Introduce key vocabulary. Generate success criteria.	 *Assessment for learning* *Literacy* *Assessment for learning*
Cognitive Conflict *Setting just the right degree of challenge.* *Problem solving*	Keep asking 'Why?' 'What if...'... Explore wrong answers. Teacher poker face in response to learner's answer. Learners challenge each other to justify points. '3*s' and an **action**. Unsolved problems notice-board.	*Assessment for learning* *Assessment for learning* *Assessment for learning*
Social Construction *Learning through talk.* *Working with others*	Thinking time/ mini-whiteboards/ basket-ball not ping pong. Small group focused talk. Emphasis on learners explaining to each other. Pole bridging. Peer assessment. Speaking frames.	*Assessment for learning* *Assessment for learning* *Literacy*
Metacognition *Thinking about strategies used and reviewing them.* *Improving own learning and performance*	Traffic lighting to gauge extent and depth of understanding. Learners come to understand external criteria for subject. Self assessment, (including successes not mentioned in success criteria). Learners decide which questions are the most difficult/ devise questions for next activity/ test etc. Learners evaluate success criteria.	*Assessment for learning* *Assessment for learning* *Assessment for learning* *Assessment for learning*
Bridging *Making links and connections within and outside school/ subject area.* *Improving own learning and performance*	Success criteria established by reading/ viewing etc. become success criteria for writing etc. Regular links to where else idea/ strategy etc. applies inside or outside school. Overall learning objective/ skill established, not just in this particular single context. Metaphors and similes.	 *Assessment for learning*

Quotations on assessment for learning and developing thinking

Approach	Developing thinking	Assessment for learning
Questioning technique	... students ... listen to and interact with one another instead of engaging in the usual "ping-pong" of teacher-student-teacher. Feuerstein 1980: 304	pupils come to realise that learning may depend less on their capacity to spot the right answer and more on their readiness to express and discuss their own understanding Black, P. et al 2002: 7
Using wrong answers	Error cannot be viewed solely as failure; rather, its source must be sought. In doing so, the teacher demonstrates his respect for the child as a thinking being who has arrived at a response through reasons that may not correspond to the task, but which, nonetheless, exist and must be explored. Feuerstein 1980: 297	By getting the pupils to share and explain their methods of solution whether or not they had got the right answer to a calculation ... teachers built up a detailed picture of pupils' strengths and weaknesses. This .. enabled the teachers to plan lessons that challenged pupils' current levels of thinking. Askew et al 1997: 38
Challenge	If cognitive conflict upsets a student's equilibrium feeling of understanding as much as he needs to, construction is the process which follows and which re-establishes equilibrium through the development of a more powerful and effective way of thinking about the problem. Adey and Shayer 1994:66	... *hard goals* have the greatest impact on performance. ...By contrast, do-one's-best goals often turn out to be not much more effective than no goals at all. Sadler 1989: 129
Peer feedback	It has been found helpful to enlist as an aide the student who finishes his work quickly. Peer tutoring is beneficial to both learners involved. The tutor should be taught, however, that to assist effectively is not to solve the problem of his neighbor, but to teach process and strategies. It is interesting to note that, because of the differential modalities and emphases of the exercises, it is not always the same child who becomes the aide. Feuerstein 1980: 304	...the interchange in peer discussions is in language that the students themselves would naturally use. Their communication with one another can use shared language forms .. so that the achievements of some can convey the meaning and value of the exercise to others still struggling... students often accept, from one another, criticisms of their work that they would not take seriously if made by their teacher. Black et al 2003: 50
Learning how to learn	(the intervention programme) produces in the organism a propensity to learn how to learn, by equipping the organism with the tools necessary for this facility. Feuerstein 1980: 25	Part of the teacher's responsibility is ... that students eventually become independent of the teacher and intelligently engage in and monitor their own development. Sadler 1989: 141

Assessment for Learning and basic skills/ key skills

Many of the following strategies help to develop oracy, a key component in developing literacy.

Assessment for learning strategy	Key skills
No hands up – all learners expected to think up an answer and be ready to express it. Thinking time; think/ pair/ share. Poker face – the teacher does not immediately reveal their reaction to an answer. Wrong answers explored. Keep asking *why?* Extended exploration of one learner's understanding at times. Learners act on feedback from teacher/ peer.	**Problem solving** *(Cognitive conflict)*
Basketball not ping-pong. Random partners. Explaining to others – benefiting others. Greens explain to reds/ ambers. Think/ pair/ share. Peer assessment.	**Working with others** *(Social construction)*
Generating success criteria/ rules for talk. Traffic lighting current understanding. Three 'stars' and an action. Explaining to others – benefiting self. Self assessment - leading to independent, autonomous learners. Evaluating success criteria against good outcomes.	**Improving own learning and performance** *(Metacognition and bridging)*

Schools which have adopted these strategies regularly report:
- increased motivation
- longer spells of engagement on tasks
- greater respect for other learners
- improved behaviour
- previously isolated/ disaffected learners becoming engaged.

It should not be inferred that independence necessarily results in learners working on their own. Part of the maturity of independence is knowing when a problem is best solved by working with others.

This kind of independence, and learning *how* to learn, is the most powerful of all multiplier effects.

Integrating assessment for learning and developing thinking

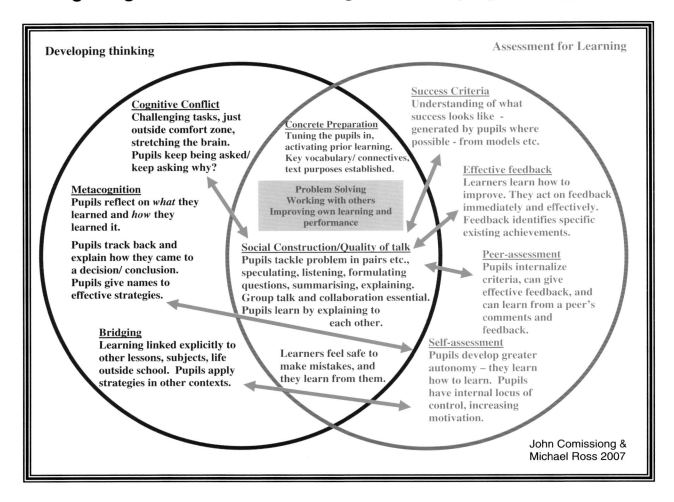

Developing thinking

Cognitive Conflict
Challenging tasks, just outside comfort zone, stretching the brain. Pupils keep being asked/ keep asking why?

Metacognition
Pupils reflect on *what* they learned and *how* they learned it.

Pupils track back and explain how they came to a decision/ conclusion. Pupils give names to effective strategies.

Bridging
Learning linked explicitly to other lessons, subjects, life outside school. Pupils apply strategies in other contexts.

Concrete Preparation
Tuning the pupils in, activating prior learning. Key vocabulary/ connectives, text purposes established.

Problem Solving
Working with others
Improving own learning and performance

Social Construction/Quality of talk
Pupils tackle problem in pairs etc., speculating, listening, formulating questions, summarising, explaining. Group talk and collaboration essential. Pupils learn by explaining to each other.

Learners feel safe to make mistakes, and they learn from them.

Success Criteria
Understanding of what success looks like - generated by pupils where possible - from models etc.

Effective feedback
Learners learn how to improve. They act on feedback immediately and effectively. Feedback identifies specific existing achievements.

Peer-assessment
Pupils internalize criteria, can give effective feedback, and can learn from a peer's comments and feedback.

Self-assessment
Pupils develop greater autonomy – they learn how to learn. Pupils have internal locus of control, increasing motivation.

John Comissiong &
Michael Ross 2007

The length of this booklet necessarily means that some ideas are given very brief treatment. It is obviously preferable if a fuller understanding is obtained by reading some of the excellent books on the topic. A selection is provided below.

Adey, P. and Shayer, M. *Learning Intelligence: Cognitive Acceleration Across the Curriculum from 5 to 15 Years* Buckingham: Open University Press

Alexander, R. (2004) *Towards Dialogic Teaching* York: Dialogos

Black, P., Wiliam, D. et al (2002) *Working inside the black box* London: King's College

Black, P., Wiliam, D. et al (2002) *Assessment for Learning: Putting it into practice* London: King's College

Feuerstein, R. (1980) *Instrumental Enrichment: an intervention program for cognitive modifiability* Baltimore: University Park Press

James, M., Black, P., Wiliam D. et al (2006) *Learning How to Learn: Tools for schools* London: Routledge

James, M. et al (2007) *Improving Learning How to Learn* London: Routledge

Mercer, N. and Littleton, K. (2007) *Dialogue and the Development of Children's Thinking* London: Routledge

Myhill, D. et al (2006) *Talking, Listening, Learning: Effective Talk in the Primary Classroom* Maidenhead: Open University Press

Watkins, C. et al (2007) *Effective Learning in Classrooms* London: Paul Chapman